£10.95

NORTHANGERLAND
Re-versioning ~~~~~~ etry
of Bran~

Branwell Brontë
&
Andrew Taylor

Leafe Press

Published by Leafe Press
Nottingham, England.
www.leafepresspoetry.com

Copyright © Andrew Taylor, 2022. All rights reserved.

ISBN: 978-1-7397213-2-9

Poems have been published in the following journals: *Anthropocene, International Times, Litter, Orbis* and *Shearsman*. Thanks to the editors.

The poems were sourced from *The Poems of Patrick Branwell Brontë* edited by Tom Winnifrith (Oxford: Basil Blackwell, 1983) and where dates were missing, cross referenced and sourced from *The Poems of Patrick Branwell Brontë A New Text and Commentary* edited by Victor A. Neufeldt (New York and London: Garland Publishing, 1990. My versions of the poems follow the ordering in the selection made by Tom Winnifrith.

The notebook poems, dating from 1847, contained in Section two of the Winnifrith book have been omitted. Cross referencing with the Neufelt text, found that many poems were drafts or versions of poems that have already been included in the first part of the Winnifrith book.

Dates sourced from the Winnifrith texts have been corrected where necessary, after consulting Neufeldt.

CONTENTS

Introduction, 7

Polar Star, 17
Thermopylae, 18
Misery Part I, 19
Misery Part II, 20
Elrington, 21
[My Ancient Ship], 22
Memory, 23
[Still and bright in twilight shining], 23
[sleep mourner sleep! - I cannot sleep], 25
[Well! I will lift my eyes once more], 26
[alone she passed the ancient hall], 27
On Caroline, 28
Caroline, 29
Harriet I, 31
Song, 33
Harriett II, 34
[Now but one moment let me stay], 36
[Oh all our cares these noontide airs], 37
Fragment, 38
[There's many a grief to shade the scene], 39
Death Triumphant, 40
Sir Henry Tunstall
        (The Wanderer), 41
Black Comb, 44
[Oh thou whose beams were most withdrawn], 45
The Triumph of Mind over Body, 46
Sonnet, 47
[Amid the world's wide din around], 48
On Landseer's Painting, 49
[The man who will not know another], 50
[The desolate earth the wintry sky], 51
[O God! while I in pleasure's wiles], 53

The Afghan War, 54
The Epicurean's Song, 55
Azrael or The Eve of Destruction, 56
The Callousness Produced by Care, 58
Peaceful death & Painful Life, 59
The Emigrant. I, 60
The Emigrant. II, 61
[I saw a picture yesterday], 62
Juan Fernandez, 63
Penmaenmawr, 64
Real Rest, 65
Sonnet, 66
[While fabled scenes & fancied forms], 67
Epistle from a Father to a Child in her Grave, 68
Morley Hall, 69
The End of All, 70
Percy Hall, 71

Bibliography and further reading, 72

For Nichola J Taylor
and
Graham Caveney

Introduction

The Brontës have been ill-served by their biographers - Juliet Barker, 1994.[1]

The days of 'Branwell-bashing' seem to be over - James Reaney.[2]

After spending time in the village of Haworth, West Yorkshire, over a period of several months between Autumn 2021 and Spring 2022, I was embroiled in the life of the place enough to understand its draw. Its most famous former residents, the Brontë family, loom large and in the minds of the many thousands of visitors, who walk the famous cobbled hill of Main Street. The attractions of the Church, Parsonage and The Black Bull Inn are, in many ways, the quintessential way of engaging with the place that the Brontës called home. One can read the literature, of course, and be swept onto the moorland beyond Haworth.

The cult of personality and biography looms large over the Brontë family. This is not the place to engage with such notions. [3]

Out of a conversation in a Nottingham city centre coffee shop in November 2021, discussing poetry and publishing, I sought to develop the idea of engaging with the poetry of Patrick Branwell Brontë. I was aware that the work of writers such as Shakespeare, Keats and Wordsworth had been engaged with in a 'collaborative' manner and wondered about the prospect of working with the poetry of Branwell Brontë. Branwell, so often overlooked and overshadowed in literary terms, by his three sisters, needs reappraisal, particularly with regards to his poetry. Even the most authoritative of critics, Juliet Barker noted back in 1994 that Branwell (as well as his father, Patrick) were due a 'fresh look.'[4] However, Branwell's work does not receive that much attention by Barker. The life appears to be of more interest than the work.

In 2017, on the anniversary of Branwell's birth (he was born on 26 June 1817) poet laureate, Simon Armitage curated an exhibition at the Brontë Parsonage Museum. Titled 'Mansions in the Sky', the exhibition's subtitle is interesting: 'The Rise and Fall of Branwell Brontë.' Armitage notes in his introduction to the exhibition catalogue that the one word that 'characterises Branwell is disappointment. He was a disappointment to others, but more painfully to himself.'[5] That Branwell was overshadowed by the successes of his sisters is not in doubt. However, there is much merit in the poetry that he produced.

Though the myths and the many inaccurate biographies have painted Branwell as a failure in terms of his writing, he was the first of the Brontës to have their writing published. *The Halifax Guardian* published a regular poetry column, and it was here, in May 1841, that a poem entitled 'Heaven and Earth' was published.[6] The poem was published under a pseudonym, Northangerland. Barker points to his diffidence 'when it came to publicly acknowledging his authorship.'[7] Branwell went onto publish 8 poems in *The Halifax Guardian*. Further poems were published in *The Leeds Intelligencer* and *The Yorkshire Gazette*.

Reading Branwell's work, I thought about how this poetry, often difficult for the modern reader in terms of its content and metre, yet full of beauty and startling imagery, was in need of a well-deserved reappraisal. A question arose about how I was to work with the poetry. Some of the work is long (and in some cases repetitive) and a judgement was made to avoid repeating motifs and produce, at times, shorter versions of the poems. I also updated archaic language, for example, substituting 'thy' for 'your'.

Taking two of John Seed's collections published by Shearsman Books, *Pictures of Mayhew: London 1850* (2005) and *That Barrikins: Pictures of Mayhew - London 1850* (2007), as my cue, I noted Seed's statement that:

"Every word in the pages that follow is drawn from Henry Mayhew's writings on London published in the Morning Chronicle from 1849 to 1850, then in 63 editions of his own weekly paper, London Labour and the London Poor between December 1850 and February 1852 and then in the four volume work of the same title."[8]

I was determined to only use Branwell's words and not add mine to the poetry. There was a temptation to update the work with a modern audience in mind. Early drafts of some of the poems did employ my own work, but I soon adjusted and followed John Seed's methodology.

If we take a look at the poem 'The Emigrant I' in full below, and compare it to my version, also reproduced, we can see an example of the process that I've made use of.

The Emigrant. I
When sink from sight the landmarks of our Home,
And – all the bitterness of farewells o'er –
We yield our spirit unto Ocean's foam,
And in the newborn life which lies before,
On far Columbian or Australian shore
Strive to exchange time past for time to come,
How melancholy then – if morn restore
(less welcome than the night's forgetful gloom)
Old England's blue hills to our sight again,
While we, our thoughts seemed weaning from her sky
The *pang* – that wakes an almost silenced pain.
Thus, when the sick man lies resigned to die,
A well-loved voice, a well remembered strain,
Lets Time break harshly on Eternity.[9]

May 28, 1845

The Emigrant. I

Sink from sight the landmarks
 of home & the bitterness
of farewells we yield spirit
to the ocean & the life before
the new born shores of Columbia
& Australia exchange past time
for time to come
 how melancholy if morning restores
(Less welcome than the night's gloom)
 Old England's harsh blue hills
while we wake to a silenced pain
like a sick man resigned
to die a well
remembered voice in eternity[10]

May 28, 1848 [May 25, 1845 in Neufeldt]
May 12, 2022

There has been a recent uplift in the number of poets engaging with poetry that have gone before. I'm thinking here of Peter Hughes' versions of Petrarch's Sonnets: *Quite Frankly: After Petrarch's Sonnets,* Philip Terry's rewriting of Shakespeare's Sonnets and Robert Sheppard's transposing of Wordsworth's Sonnets.[11] Sheppard notes the terminology of this kind of work: 'transposed, overdubbed, 'translated' and 're-fitted' and goes on to suggest that this is a form of writing that will continue: "Of course, I know that other people have […] before me (and I'm pretty convinced they will after me, as I now turn away from these procedures)."[12]

Determining the nature of the poems collected in *Northangerland* is tough. Partly I see them as collaborations with a silent partner. Having previously collaborated with poets Charlie Baylis and Nick Power, this work undoubtedly feels different.[13] There is an unwritten contract between collaborative writers as the collaboration advances and of course, there is the call and response notion of actively working through a project together. During my time in Haworth, I visited the Brontë Parsonage several times, the church, and The Black Bull Inn, where Branwell drank. Part of this was designed to inhabit aspects of Branwell's world, albeit to an extent, in facsimile mode.

Looking past Sheppard's definitions to the cut-up methods employed by the Dadaists and initiated by Tristan Tzara and later used by writers such as William Burroughs, I knew that this mode of working would somehow not be correct for my engagement with Branwell's work. 'Cutting up' the work in this way, though, would certainly have made for some interesting results. Partly, my aim, as noted above, was to revitalise the work for the modern reader. I like the notion of creating 're-versions' of the poems and taking that what has gone before and engaging with previously extant work, to produce new poems.

This act of 're-versioning' or re-enacting of Branwell's work gave rise to some interesting results that I hope those who are familiar with the original work will enjoy, as well as those coming to the poetry of Branwell Brontë for the first time.

Andrew Taylor
Nottingham, Summer 2022.

REFERENCES

1. Juliet Barker, *The Brontës*, (London: Weidenfeld & Nicolson, 1994) pp. xix-xx.
2. James C. Reaney, 'A Fresh Look at Patrick Branwell Brontë: the Prose', *Brontë Studies*, 26.1 (April 2001), 1-9 (p. 1)
3. See the bibliography for further details of material related to the lives of the Brontë family.
4. Barker, p.xx.
5. Simon Armitage, *The Rise and Fall of Branwell Brontë* (Haworth: Brontë Society, 2017) p.8.
6. Barker, pp.497-8. Though the poem appears in Neufeldt, Winnifrith doesn't include it. He does make clear that his book is not a complete collection of Branwell's poetry.
7. Barker, p.497.
8. John Seed, author's note in *That Barrikins: Pictures of Mayhew - London 1850* (Exeter: Shearsman Books, 2007), p.5
9. Branwell Brontë, 'The Emigrant I' in *The Poems of Patrick Branwell Brontë* edited by Tom Winnifrith (Oxford: Basil Blackwell, 1983), p. 361
10. See p. 61 for the version of 'The Emigrant I' in isolation.
11. Peter Hughes, *Quite Frankly: After Petrarch's Sonnets* (St. Leonards on Sea: Reality Street, 2015). Robert Sheppard
12. Robert Sheppard, 'Wordsworth's Sonnets Transposed for the 21st Century appears on Zwiebelfish!' (2022) < http://robertsheppard.blogspot.com/2022/07/robert-sheppard-wordsworths-sonnets.html> [Accessed 18th July 2022] (para 1 of 7). Sheppard has also written versions of poems by Shelley, Keats, Mary Robinson and Hartley Coleridge, amongst others. Philip Terry, *Shakespeare's Sonnets* (Manchester: Carcanet, 2011)
13. I've collaborated with two poets, Charlie Baylis and Nick Power. The texts produced are Charlie Baylis and Andrew Taylor, *at first it felt like flying* (Beaworthy: Indigo Dreams, 2019) and Nick Power and Andrew Taylor, *Lowdeine Chronicles* (Liverpool: erbacce Press, 2019).

Thanks to Alan Baker at Leafe Press for initiating the conversation about what to *do* with Branwell's poems and publishing them. Thanks also to Charlie Baylis, Sam Buchan-Watts, Alex Byron, Linda Kemp, Nick Power, Robert Sheppard, Rachel Smith, Helen Tookey, Cliff Yates, Tim Youngs and Rory Waterman for their continued support and enthusiasm for what I do.

NORTHANGERLAND

Polar Star

Heaven of northern fields
    May light
sing praises
Sordid flatterers cringe
before the rich man
& bow
& bring their offerings

But on some high
hanging rock
tempests fly
across a midnight sky
shining bright & silent

Star of the pole
how many look
wandering
    abyss of air
rent & riven
black clouds
    increasing shrouds
with surf shaken shore
as they drive secret quicksands
& dark blue concave of night
a thousand stars fixed
a silent sky native shores

Ocean roam
        waste on waste
native valley lies
bitter blast inclement sky
everlasting guide

June 26th 1832 - Branwell Brontë
March 20th 2022 - Andrew Taylor

Thermopylae

Morning rise
above the sea
heaven returning light
hill & valley plain
the iron shroud of night
awake awake
the sunlit dawn
waves in glittering light
golden lustre glow

August 9th 1834
March 21st 2022

Misery Part I

Bare & groaning boughs
very energy of soul
mystery undefined
soft & calm

December 18, 1835
March 20, 2022

Misery Part II

Wild winds sighing
dark its evening ray
drives past cold
&
drenching showers
of sleety spray

Sigh of the wild blast
       the heath bends
wails & wanders of wintry sound
longdrawn strain
battle with the setting sun

The chill approach
demands a sterner care
torrent chafe streamlet
curling

Battered cell still life
& soul memory dwell
wilder power

From such a present
turns to what has been
strained thoughts
to reach its strand

Reason's last spark
one short broken gasp
& a dream is existence flying

March 2, 1836
March 23, 2022

Elrington

Unvaried light
city of the sea
sunshine of a summer's sun
fetes & feasts
& ethereal music

May 17, 1836
March 23, 2022

These lines were attributed to Emily Brontë in *The Complete Poems of Emily Brontë*, edited by Clement K.Shorter, 1910 - Tom Winnifrith.

[My Ancient Ship]

Ancient sea who is gone?
unknowing what fate may be
native world of tempests
lost like a speck

southern waters restless
rolling wilder with every vision
of shore those eternal waves
which surge below

a thought that colours all
a melancholy shade-like pall
cast from from the vast city
hut & temple sharing same light

For years through youthful hope
for years a sea without a breeze
for years silent sleepless care

Not a wanderer over the Atlantic
main visions rest in woodlands
of the west

July, 1836.
March, 2022.

Memory

Magic fingers
a wild & passing
thrill
the chord spirit
lingers
sleeping silently
days of changeless
pain
the air slept
silence

July, 1836
March, 2022

[Still and bright in twilight shining]

Glitters the evening star
    closing rosebuds
shed their fragrance
the river pales
    slumber near
solemn silence
        the fading day

hush of sacred sadness
weary wild
        sweep of trees
beneath the power of
twilight's frown
wide west decline
& celestial sympathy

Soft & sweet the silver beam
        through the bower
bright drops
unnoticed break

August 13, 1836.
March 25, 2022.

[sleep mourner sleep! - I cannot sleep]

Weary mind wanders
silent weep

eyes turned to stone
footsteps find a rest

could the world lapse
in days?

Consecrate grief
prospect of relief alone

in sunshine
I cannot forget the years

of scenes & times
voices tuned to

music's thrill
cannot awaken gladness

sweep the strings
no sound will rouse stirless air

Evening's latest ray
from wild heaven is flown

January 13, 1837.
March 27, 2022.

[Well! I will lift my eyes once more]

Western heaven closed
        sever thoughts wild world of misery
bright journeyer companion of dark
        decline behind native flee following west

Native home memory lost in unclouded blaze
        central light crowns dim hills though life
is waning low heart expanding
        lips frame farewell smile celestial glow

summer clouds sunlit trees blackbird's song
        bed of farewell pain wildered maze
dreamlike skies strange unsteady light
        know not the reality lost bird stormy sea

no hope in that dark air homeward through
        that wintry sky return lost bird return
glimpses of a spirit shore strength of eyesight
        to seize the falling rein through dreams

with feigned reality tossed & fevered bed
        mirror broken on grass wild dreams of western
skies & shattered memories glitter through
        the gloam in cold decay unclouded light

decline glistening gaze golden in the gleam
        as the wild winds sink in peace glorious
skies dreamy depths of azure blue sunset isles
        of paradise in cloud land

February 9, 1837.
March 27, 2022.

[alone she passed the ancient hall]

while night hung around
              silent echoless
windows arched on high
in midnight's cheerless vacancy
winged with fear four clasped hands
give her spirit to the hour

Ghostly meaning
              phantom pain
the sun might show more bright
than sorrow's future history
earthly aid unmoored over life's
wide ocean

Vain relief burning brow
              back to
the declining beam to night
be slow in step & soft in tread
sleep mouldering on amid the yell

the first dawn of summer morn
              skylark's song
of love an answer to the blackbird's
song the earliest sounds
that greet the morn

March 1 1837
March 30 2022

On Caroline

Light of ancestral hall
  palace for a pall garden

to aisles & eternal sleep
  mute & motionless

Slow midnight moments
  to morning's beam

churchyard stone can
  hide past smiles

memory with her soul
  joy itself has flown

1837
2022

Caroline

Clear & calm the declining day
brightness to the air
sunshine shining slanted
    shadows stretching
hush of advancing eve
rest is near

such a silence given
the voice of nature
quiet airs sacred gladness
    breathing through woodlands
wild the whirl of mortal
madness music making

Pearly sky oak trees huge
on high echoes when autumn
winds are strongest
    a funeral bell
life's uncertain day like lifeless
nature roll back & memory's light

Into a harmony sweet & solemn
the magic glass dream
strange shadows
    with defined forms
serene shining skies blue hills
& green groves

flowers long since dead
budded bloomed & gone
she who loved it was not there
    her favourite rosebud
the sunny hush of afternoon
passed slowly & sedately on

Quiet uncertain fears
downcast eyes & brows of gloom
the sickening chill
        in the dear folds of embrace
in mild & magical delight
the marble cheek tears of anguish

That one glimpse of eternity
how bitter seemed that moment
when glitter was to turn to rust
        cold of damp sepulchral
air lingering sadly & serene
a last farewell

& fade while the midnight wind
brought back the hours
of wild December weather
        chords of inward thought
rehearsing some
remembered strain

1837
2022

Harriet I

How Edenlike
where youth
& beauty join to waken
with looks & divine smiles
free from care

In summer's pride
beams of imperial
blaze & yet so tender
departed spirits glide
sunset skies of the mind

Power & pleasure reign
the starless night
glittering mazes blaze
of light senses stealing
sights away

Of life's most Northern
stage years of corroding
pain power to assuage
the troubles heal the
troubled heart

in such a magic hour
the full heart & thrilling
eye like evening sun
over a hill splendour
of that sunny brow

One vision seems to glow
beneath the lights on high
perfumed air sighs so sweetly
these stealing footsteps
tumultuous melody

chords abrupt & loud
subsiding mournfully a
sudden welcome in tones
that sound familiar
banisher of misery

It seems the past can shine
time has marked with care
ships in harboured rest will rot
sooner than those whose tattered
sails have braved wild waves

Every hour of happier skies
& brighter weather will revive
memories other hours of vanished
bliss a look of double meaning
& a strange smile of treachery

August 27th 1837 (beginning)
November 1837 (end)
April 5th 2022

Song

As time leaves years behind
life's ever changing

space severs heart from heart
first love bids youthful memories

fresh affection deeper fountains
spring feelings

single moment pressed softly
flowers such a constant joy

impassioned tide ill designed
little cared for but the hour

was gratified summer skies &
sunny smiles shade severe

solemn sweetness deluge of
distress to join the broken chain

& wake the ancient flame
turn to that magic sound

that busy hum of social sound
mirrors mimics nature

Time's warning finger a score
of years departing starless nights

August 27-November 9, 1837.
April 5-April 8, 2022.

Harriett II

At dead of midnight dreams
       of dread shore gasped breathless

shattered senses
short short in fevered slumber
another hour that night might
number deeply veiled in eternal
gloom

That awful void yawns
          the joys once enjoyed

That look
& hear the dread command
Archangels can shrink terrors
the face the form scarce
vanished glorious star

Wild hopes of future union
     dead to shame the misery of disgrace

Sit & silently
weep the whole world seemed
asleep conscience came to
gnaw with ceaseless flame
until day & night has flown

A thousand lights beaming down
     the wide world holds still

Wait through the waning
     night until the first pale hue

May 14, 1838
April 9, 2022

[Now but one moment let me stay]

One hour calm on the brink
on Evesham's woody brow

sullen sound sullen roll bursts
over many a parting soul

shade of scarce quiet trees
sweet evening breeze a breath

& nothing in the twilight sky
all calm & grey slow sounding

uncertain strange heard by all
round the wall a murmuring

Summer 1837
April 9 2022

[Oh all our cares these noontide airs]

Glad & bright sight appears
each sound so soft
through the shade of the glade
leaves are dancing
a hundred plumes beyond
the myrtle grove
this lonely spot retires
among its trees not noticed

July/August 1836
11th April 2022

Fragment

Heartsick at scenes of death
with its customed gift of farewell
light through the paths of night
 battle smoke with shrieks
of mortal pain

The moon her mild face shines
as hurrying clouds disclosed
one divine beam sleet & shower
 intervened & darkness
veiled the scenes

January 23, 1838
April 11, 2022

[There's many a grief to shade the scene]

hide the starry skies
from mortal life
the storms of sorrow
& art shining on

January 23, 1838
April 11, 2022

Death Triumphant

Oh! on this first bright morn
that seems to change wild
winter feel the freshness

spreading glad light long
delayed sweet woodland
sunshine wake of memory

May they bud with promise
of summer beneath
the morning sun

forms refuse the real
& unreal to confuse phantom
path of joys

May, 1838.
April, 2022.

Sir Henry Tunstall
(The Wanderer)

It's only afternoon but midnight's gloom
could scarcely seem stiller in the dark
room in the ancient mansion slow ticking
of the clock & away the woodland
waterfall sounds lost like noonday stars
the group look to the threatening
    weather
grey clouds gather over moveless trees
long hope bursting into morn

• • • • •

  rooks and doves hover round
flowers planted past seasons have
drooped voiceless farewells parting
scene 'how soon he'd come again'
calmness a last embrace swift over
the pavement eyes fixed on air checkered
sunshine & the open field sat together till
the twilight dim but all the world seemed
gone with him

• • • • •

  windows opening on twilight air silently
thinking of afar climes beneath the
evening star dear as a friend our wood
our house ourselves were not the same as
those that floated through boyhood dreams
    storms & summers dull heavens
feverish hope to chase full of honours
fresh tidings of fame lose sighs of grief
in smiles of joy murmur sound of rapid

wheels hasty din what pales each cheek
what lights each swimming eye?

• • • • •

the start of mute surprise long embrace
eloquent silence all is surrounded by the
light of dreams dissolved in tears eyes dim
to present joys the cloud of memories &
the iron hoar of time a look a tone can
sometimes bring the past it was Henry! It was their own!

His restless glances roam as if he
couldn't find his home long-lost face
darkened by clime not pain a steadier tone
of spirits & ancient wildered view the
twilight hour appears a summing-up of
daylight's toils & grief

• • • • •

That dull hour darkened & bore the
breeze in mournful murmurs & promise of
a storm no candle to cheat its gloom in
sleep unstained by sorrow wrecks of time
when all the world looked young old
affection is an empty name nothing we
loved remains the same

• • • • •

Like one heart-sick it was a bitter task &
showed the wreck of years a book known
before a hand lightly traced

• • • • •

Long over the darkening page Henry
pondered time-worn words sent to him
from the grave as if heaven spoke from
the winter fireside sadly pale angel
eyes voiceless calm silent hope that
gladdened past 'well world oh world!'
you've given me my destiny the eye that
glistened with delightful tears

   One pale star above the sombre trees
when all else darkened brightening the sky
over life's waters should glisten Memory's Star

April 15, 1840.
April 15, 2022.

Black Comb

Far off & half revealed
light & shade
      Black Comb half smiles
half frowns his form
bending into peace
a thousand years of struggle
subdued bask in warm sunshine
his heath-clad height doesn't tower
over this world's sympathies
tempests find Black Comb invincible
we are lost & should know life so well

1840
2022

[Oh thou whose beams were most withdrawn]

Frowning at earliest dawn foretold
the storms hour on hour passed

Blasts of bleak December & tempests
unsmiling storms

Twilight's dark decline roll back
the clouds a single silver line

Prayer is earnest a short space of rest
before home to dust & worms

A single gleam of light amid darkness
of churchyard night

Oppressed with pain mind beneath
despair your wrath void of power

Fight or flee to avert your eye with
sunken heart & supplicant knee

Former life strife to strife passes over
the bewildering scene

Every power & you have given much
spent in the present hour

never turned my God to you
still I laughed at peace & rest

August 8, 1841
April 18, 2022

The Triumph of Mind over Body

Man thinks too often of the ills of life
    ceaseless labour & its causeless
strife when dark waves roll round the body
the soul struggling it can never triumph
    or feel free while pain & poverty binds

No words have power to rouse the brain
    oppressed with grief bowed with pain
none will hear how high man's soul
can soar over body's misery worn-out
    a single syllable silence broken

Nights of sleepless pain or toilsome days
    feeble frame tread the footsteps of
the bold & strong born beneath a lowly
star like a lamb lost upon a gloomy moor
    like one flower tossed leagues from shore

Ceaseless showers obscure the misty vale
    Winter winds wail swollen stream rushing
wild nothing impossible to steadfast will now
wave the wand again
    England's shore through smoke

1842
2022

Sonnet

earth-born
cares bind
chains faint & feeble
soul storm struck
pain & poverty
& want
sadness ends
its years
mortal gloom
garret
hunger creeps
darksome
as a
dreaded tomb

September 3, 1841.
April 18, 2022.

[Amid the world's wide din around]

from far a solemn sound
  still dear to you
since light given to your soul
& glow of heaven to your earth

not a voice from ruby lips
    & sapphire eyes not echoed
from sensual joys when I heard
it amid town-like bustle

Beneath the thundering
  of passing engines
& the approaching train
to startle apathy

Time left so long behind
  Summer afternoons
basking beneath a glorious sky
a noble page to break the monotony

Withered heath & windless hill
  revealed a world of wild wonders
bold & divine scenes beyond the
horizon's line

September 11, 1841.
April 18, 2022.

On Landseer's Painting

Fame's beams dry affection's tears
those who rise forget from where
    they spring
Wealth's golden glories all that our
    hope seeks & caution fears
destroy holy thoughts joys & cares
deemed so grovelling power nor pride
are yours

April 28, 1842
April 19, 2022

[The man who will not know another]

Who loves not comrade
friend or brother
frozen eye bloodless heart
nature repugnant
bids depart

Born for nobler aim
your task to shun such
shame & never think
who gives courtesy
a hand

However mean a man
may be know man is man
however high your gentle
line he who writes can
rank with you

Some light still glitters
mind flies restless nights
& troubled days never
slight instinct
with noble sympathies

1841
2022

[The desolate earth the wintry sky]

Ceaseless rain showers
    the farewell of the year
drear the sight & sad
the sound wailing bitter winds

December's wind as it moans
brings varied thoughts to mind
its storm drenched wing
    of words not said

When the green hills & leaves
are bright in noonday night
    the present only lives
but when my chimnies roar

the feeble present loses power
mighty past survives

As roses blow & streams gently flow
I cannot think of anything but
childhood happiness
of unshadowed joys
or faces made to love

Like nature's funeral
    when winter evenings fall
    the soul gets strength
its thoughts will & power to rise
above the present day

Recall the mind's victories
    over bitter heavens stormy winds
& all the wars of humankind
dungeon's gloom could not becloud

those eyes that revealed mighty
London & one poor man
   seated alone owned by poverty

a thousand unknown worlds
   of light that left this world behind
though poor neglected blind & old
misery must bow to mind

December 15, 1841
April 19, 2022

[O God! while I in pleasure's wiles]

count years & hours as one
    & wrapped in pleasure joys
can never be done

sustaining power
    to look to the past
& the shadowed hour

stretch this hand a last adieu
    sad friends that round
no more

the bright hours lead
    on the present passage
join the silent dead

cease to seek the light
    the evening heaven
direct through death's dark night

December 19, 1841.
April 20, 2022.

The Afghan War

Winds thunder rain
shakes each pane

our hearts glide gently
remember mid woe

funeral bell toll mourning
hour no returning

restore round hearthstones
ear scarce conscious

Winter's war outside
man chilly silence dying

ceases story song & smile
doubtings vanish

ancient England a dead
host inglorious & cruel

May 7th 1842
April 22nd 2022

The Epicurean's Song

Sorrow visits why
should we mourn?

tomorrow's sun
will have departed

beat for a moment
which cannot return

Time has taken each
hour & they never awaken

We may defy shadows
like memory fleeting

as midsummer wave
gather flowers

mournful or pleasant
it's all that is ours

Vanishing hours follow
fast change is the only thing

always continuing sweep
creation with its tide

July 2nd & 4th 1842
April 22nd 2022

Azrael or The Eve of Destruction

Brothers & men stay
    beside the latest grave
underneath this nameless sod
hands with mine laid today

Dissolve the chain a whisper
    on the wind
dark doom blinded victims
find wilder storms within

Forgive the accents break
    shall nature die?
forgive that pause a look
to heaven for earth's peace

alone no joy latest beam
    angel's presence
starless night beginning
of an end

Knell of iron from the skies
    none returned from earth
to embitter human joys
on life's lettered page

Dim eyes darkness in day
    age thinks the past bright
memory fails from truth to
error with a nod

Trust reason believe the
    vast canopy overhead
believe that hoar descending
hairs are more sage

than a fruitful forest tree
    rotting planks & a
thought for Earth gazing
at the skies

July / August 1842
April 2022

The Callousness Produced by Care

Young eyes fullest of tears
  & why do the youthful often sigh
when friends forsake
  or dangers awaken fears?
he has seen the springtide
  & time's rough voice
increase of days increases misery
  & misery brings selfishness
which sears the heart's feelings
  in death's grasp the eyes are blind
to others' pains so whose hopes are over
  turn coldy from mankind's suffering
a bleeding spirit will delight in gore
  a tortured heart will make the mind a tyrant

May 5 & 7 1842
May 1 & 2 2022

Peaceful death and Painful Life

Why do we sorrow for the happy dead?
  their life is lost toil is over
want shall trouble them no more
  earthly bed now they sleep
in the dark chambers night &
  silence seal each guarded door
so turn from such & mourn the
  dead whose spirit flies whose life
departs before death has come
who finds no heaven beyond
                          gloomy skies

June 2 & 4 1842
May 2 & 8 2022

The Emigrant. I

Sink from sight the landmarks
  of home & the bitterness
of farewells we yield spirit
to the ocean & the life before
the new born shores of Columbia
& Australia exchange past time
for time to come
  how melancholy if morning restores
(Less welcome than the night's gloom)
  Old England's harsh blue hills
while we wake to a silenced pain
like a sick man resigned
to die a well
remembered voice in eternity

May 28, 1848 [May 25, 1845 in Neufeldt]
May 12, 2022

The Emigrant. II

When after a long day consumed
  in toil under the welcome shade
of trees thanklessly upturning England's
 soil the lonely exile seeks his evening
ease it's not the woods the spirit
sees nor calms the world's turmoil
or cools the spicy burning brow
  No! The gusty clouds of the feverish Isle
brings music on the stormy wind
  lower shadows & night's darkness
calls to mind a demon thirst & feverish
  sleep when the wanderer bows & feels
the cooling shower
                    & hears the rushing rill

May 1845
May 2022

[I saw a picture yesterday]

of him who died for me which
struggled to display mortal agony

Today I saw a pencil drawn picture
which gave midnight hues to morn

Effort to contradict meaning where
sunshine should be painting shade

keep the hue of happy light that
shines from summer's skies

Give calm to one whose heart
has banished toil from mine

1844/45
2022

Juan Fernandez

Lonely speck ocean's waste
hope of rest to come
beneath a boiling sea
greeting cup to fill
in each gale hope's whispers
breathe

happiness unnoticed drift us
toward despair bane
    of our distress
flowered scents the sailor loves
   salt wind from the Main
sweet wind from the healing shore

grains to them worth more than gold

Frowned over England's hostile
shore
    gilt fairy-like a thousand rills
in salt waves lost eyes
death's films might restore
    to gaze melancholy
weakness fade tossed like a withered
leaf nature's power to point the mental sight

1846/7
26 May 2022

Penmaenmawr

November's clouds winds & chill
bring your tempest-beaten
form to look at a dreary sky
as late they look on your sublimity
as troubled as the restless sea I
found in the waves companionship
amid tears I watched you blue
over the ocean's roar & over retiring
fields echoed in mournful tones
waves clouds & shadows in restless
change that old fort scattered grey
boulders

Penmaenmawr through all its shades
has no memory of when Britain rested
on your giant power no feeling for the
verdant slope chequered pastures
overwhelming charm of the old ocean
unshaken realm roar hurls echo back
to old Mona's shore my angel's mind that
clung to Ouse's fertile side objectless on
Menai's tide oh mighty hill communion
of vague unity to endure yet never feel
peace all woes sustain yet never know
despair stand through storm & shine
                                          Penmaenmawr!

November 1845
May 2022

Real Rest

The corpse on the water eyes turned
arms outstretched wave on wave
upbears boundlessly ocean thins
its flowing decay not sorrow seas are milder
than this world's turmoil corruption
robs its cheeks of red wounded vanity
grieves with untormented eye heart &
brain suffering floats across the main
love & joy have perished worms & weeds
hide beauty in a voyage for eternity
though naked the corpse feels not poverty
nor knows distress

What scenes of sorrow has it left behind
how sad the breathing life how free
from strife the sojourn with the dead
a world-wide wanderer over the waves
the heart beats bursting veins absence
doesn't break a chain no sudden agonies
all men covert REAL REST warm with
young life not cold in death's decline
an eye that sees the light of Heaven
a thrilled & pleasured heart gift of oblivion's
healing balm share the slumbers
in the ocean tomb

1845-1846
2022

Sonnet

With cheerful hours gone
that caused body & mind
to nourish love & friendship
for our kind our souls to sever
from life's light there still may be
some pillow to bosom
to heartily deliver toward death's
dreary road our darling's feet
should tread each step to draw our
own steps to the same abode
& make a festival of sepulture
for joy & joy owed to us
should death frighten us when
he would restore her?

April, 1846 (Autumn 1846 - Neufeldt)
June, 2022

[While fabled scenes & fancied forms]

& leanings on thoughts
  with visionary calm
strive to cheat memory
  still before the inward eye
the sunbeam shines far
  and amid December's dreary
sky gives comfort to a wanderer
  hardly *comfort* that speaks
too much of security & peace
  long unheard resigned
for one glimpse in the far light

Late 1845/early 1846
June 14 2022

Epistle from a Father to a Child in her Grave

Life-reviving April showers hide
withered grass beneath Springtide
flowers & gives promise of rich
                fields & forests

I write what you will never read
for when you died your day was
in its dawn childhood's twilight star
       illuminated sweet & feeble

If you'd have seen a summer sea
   skies of azure blue & waters green
melting to mist amid the sheen
   you'd never believe what it was to live

Nature like a map winding river tree
     town & tower in shadow
& sunlight restlessness & worrying
     so sure your lot is brighter

April 3, 1846.
July 16, 2022.

Morley Hall
Leigh, Lancashire

Life's overcast youth that come
like funeral-following crowds

weary of a sunbeam burst
that casts away woes

borrow brighter joys fields
of June with May Day flowers

flowering meadows fiery flash
& bursting peal

robbed of all having bright
examples by head or hand

wide Lancashire has changed
wonder of Liverpool & Manchester

youth killed by toil & profits
bought with lives

Summer wind sang round halls
engine's steam like dew from

waterfalls pine for green fields
Lancashire's brick built houses

& factories wrecks fast vanishing

1846-1847
14 June 2022

The End of All

In that unpitying night
    by fire's declining
light silent sighted
    grief's bitter tide
earthly hope each clock strike
the still chamber anguish room

the tomb's eternal shade
    sickening fear
shadow spread of tears
long howl of winter's wind
wild waves   wandered
unconfined & far off
surging   peace

Vast December sea
    revealed solitary liberty
draw back the curtains
sweep the waves of Norway's main
track the sands of Syria

Wildly ride pressed coldly down
    take an opiate
dream with a heart-wrung
groan of bright heaven
        & paradise

June 5, 1847
June 18, 2022

Percy Hall

Westering sunbeams smiled
green leaves glittered
where Mary sat
to feel the summer breeze
through June's long afternoons
face fanned by summer evening's air

Lost in dreams debarred from sleep
creeps in a feverish heat weariness
& listlessness stately woods float before
commingled with cloud
snatching short glimpses in day dreams
& labyrinth of thought

However dim the dream indefinable
fleeting the future whispering farewell
holy sunlight angelic bloom glorious
world beyond over the glowing green
silent tread toward the shining sky
& feverish smiles decked with flowers

1847
2022

Bibliography and further reading

(Armitage, Simon) *The Rise and Fall of Branwell Brontë* (Haworth: Brontë Society, 2017)

Barker, Juliet, *The Brontës,* (London: Weidenfeld & Nicolson, 1994)

Brontë, Emily Jane, Ed. Janet Gezari, *The Complete Poems,* (London: Penguin, 1992)

Du Maurier, Daphne, *The Infernal World of Branwell Brontë* (Harmondsworth: Penguin Books, 1972)

Kelly, James T, *The Life and Work of Branwell Brontë* (Norwich: Skerry Books, 2020)

Law, Alice, *Patrick Branwell Brontë* (London: A.M. Philpot, 1923)

Neufeldt, Victor A.,ed. *The Poems of Patrick Branwell Brontë: A New Text and Commentary* (New York and London: Garland Publishing, 1990.

Rees, Joan, *Profligate Son: Branwell Brontë and his Sisters* (London: Robert Hale, 1986)

Winnifrith, Tom, ed. *The Poems of Patrick Branwell Brontë* (Oxford: Basil Blackwell, 1983)

Lightning Source UK Ltd.
Milton Keynes UK
UKHW011030041022
409906UK00004B/92